Cows and Calves

by Ann-Marie Kishel

first step nonfiction

Lerner Publications Company · Minneapolis

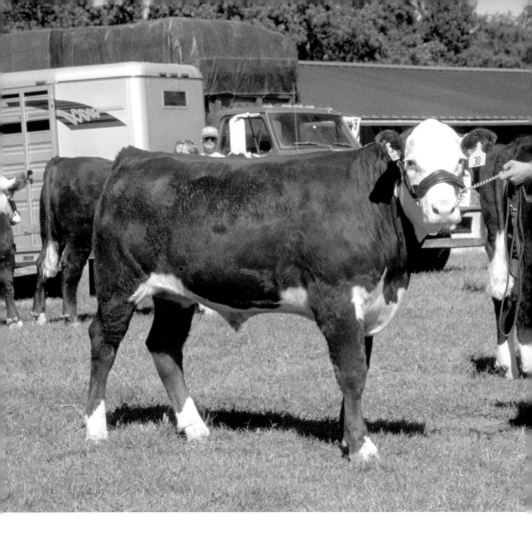

A cow has four legs.

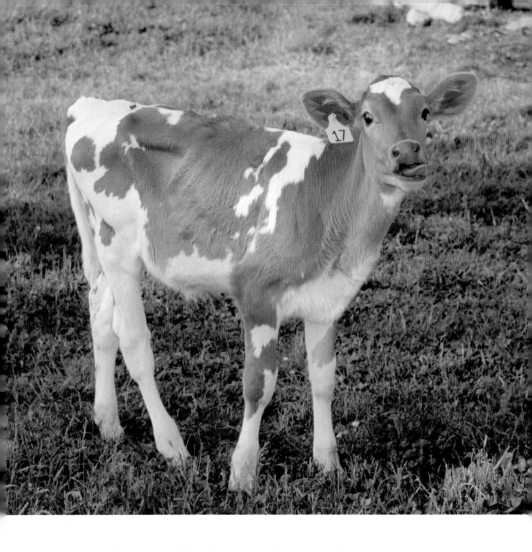

A calf has four legs.

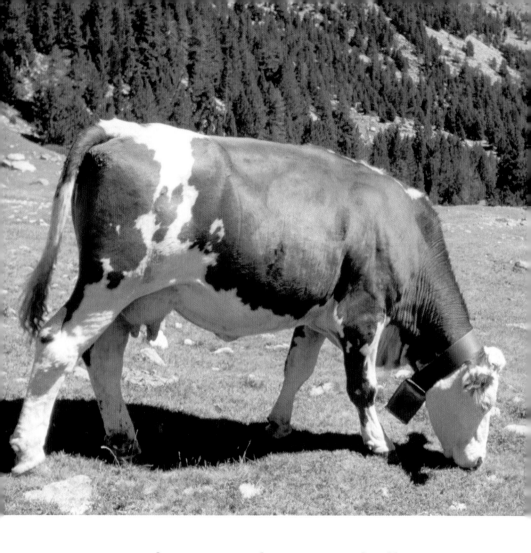

A cow has a tail.

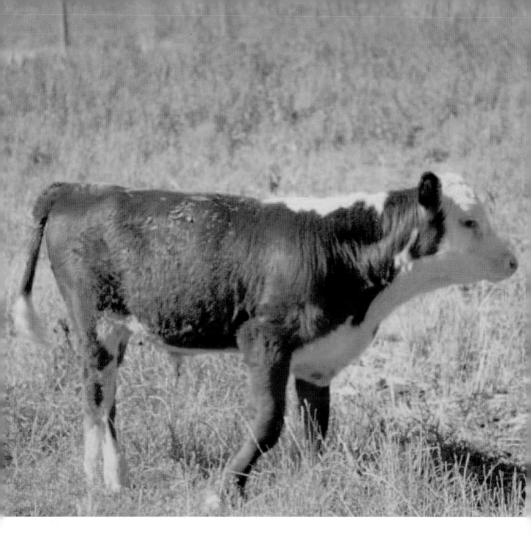

A calf has a tail.

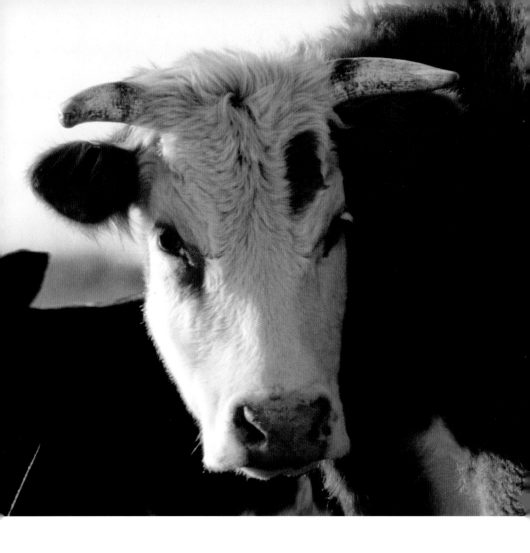

A cow has ears.

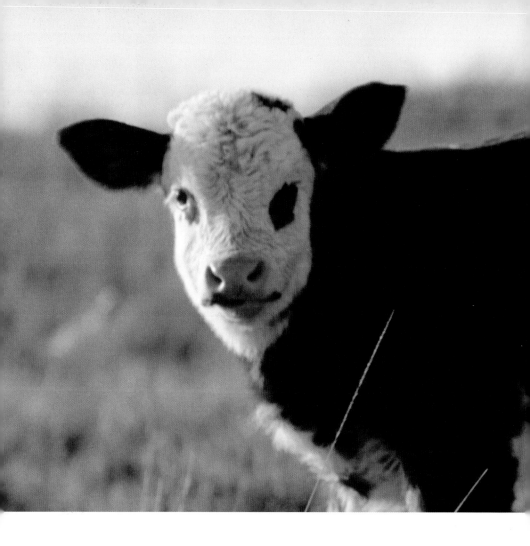

A calf has ears.

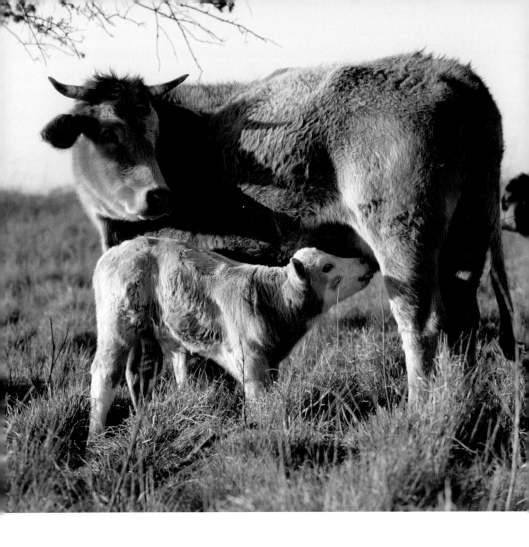

Cows and calves are alike.